GOD
AS WOMAN,
WOMAN
AS GOD

God
as Woman,
Woman
as God

J. Edgar Bruns

PAULIST PRESS
New York/Paramus/Toronto

Copyright © 1973 by
The Missionary Society
of St. Paul the Apostle
in the State of New York

Library of Congress
Catalog Card Number: 73-75247

ISBN 0-8091-1771-1

Published by Paulist Press
Editorial Office: 1865 Broadway, N.Y., N.Y. 10023
Business Office: 400 Sette Drive, Paramus, N.J. 07652

Printed and bound in the
United States of America

Contents

For my sister

Preface

I regard this little study—which is not directed to specialists of any sort—as a broad phenomenological survey of the relationship between the two notions of woman and God in the history of Western religious tradition. It is particularly in this tradition that male, patriarchal rule and authority have been dominant in historical times, and it seems worthwhile, accordingly, to examine the religious literature of this tradition in order to ascertain whether or not the female was truly subdued even at the highest level, that of ideology. It is my thesis that she was not and that, repeatedly, woman asserts her equality if not her superiority to the male. As will become apparent, I find one theme dominant throughout the material chosen: the equation of woman with intelligence and civilization. That this *is* a major theme of the ancient mythologies and of later, even Christian developments, cannot, I think, be denied. It seems particularly worthwhile to take note of this because our history, which means our social development, certainly has not encouraged such a view, and I suggest that the reasons for this lie buried in the transitional period between history and pre-history. But religion embraces all the racial memories of man, and convictions established long before the art of writing are free to well-up and create the paradoxes that we find in the sacred books of the West. It also seems to me that this is a particularly felicitous theme to ponder in a period when woman has become especially conscious of and apprehensive about her role in society. If my thesis is correct at all, it suggests that right along the male has seen woman as more intelligent (which is, of course, not to be equated with "educated") than himself and that the projection of the female as a mere sex object is at least partly a fiction designed to veil his fear that she is, in a civilized world, his foremost competitor.

Since this is a phenomenological study, all religious symbols of "the divine woman" have been treated alike. This may offend some believing Christians for whom it will seem next to blasphemy to consider the Virgin Mary in the same light as, for example, Isis, but it should not. To quote John Henry Newman, it is wrong to say: "These things are in heathenism, therefore they are not Christian." The informed Christian view is that if "these things are in Christianity," then on that account "they are not heathen" because "one special way in which Providence has imparted divine knowledge to us has been by enabling (the Church) to draw and collect it together out of the world" (*Milman's View of Christianity*). It is this view, I think, which, on a different level, the psychologist, the anthropologist, and the sociologist of religion would accept and commend. In any case the endeavor here is to understand how man has dealt with the two concepts of God and woman from the viewpoint of an outside observer, illusory as that aim may be.

The bibliographies appended to the sections of the book represent suggested readings. In some cases I have relied on these works for information, but in many instances I have included them simply because they deal with the same topic or topics. Often my own views and deductions differ considerably from those of the authors cited.

Part One

The Earliest World

I

Did earliest man think of God as a woman, specifically as a great mother? The question is raised because among the more numerous artifacts of pre-historic man is the figure, seated or standing, of an extraordinarily obese woman. The most famous of these is the so-called Venus of Willendorf to which we can add her sisters from Gogarino and, more recently, those discovered at Çatal Hüyük. Before answering the question we must bear in mind that we really have no knowledge at all, and never will, about *earliest* man's religious views. Of *earliest* man we know only that he made tools (*homo faber*) and we take this to be a sign that his intelligence was human. In recent years even this assumption has been questioned. Burial of the dead is viewed as a more definitive indication of humanity, and it certainly distinguishes man from other animals. Many see in burial the earliest signs of a developing religious sense and this may well be true, but of course it does not tell us what God or gods accompanied it. Only in his artistic efforts has pre-literate man given us the kind of material on which to construct hypotheses about such things as his religion. They can never be more than hypotheses because he has not left us his own interpretation of the scenes and figures he created; that could only be done in writing, and it is precisely because he did not write that pre-literate man remains pre-historic. With our modern techniques we can date ancient artifacts with reasonable accuracy, so that, in a sense, any human remains can be located in time. Pre-historic man is not, then, a-historic as though we had no idea of when he lived (other than that it was more than eight or ten thousand years ago), nor is he pre-historic in the sense that we know nothing about him, for we can indeed reconstruct his world, depending upon the number of vestiges he has left behind and the geological strata in which they are found; but he *is* pre-historic in the sense that he has not *told us* what he thought of the things he wrought nor who wrought them nor why they were wrought (in some cases, of course, the reason is self-evident: a knife is made to cut, a bowl to contain, etc., but a figurine?).

Among archaeologists and historians of religion the predominating hypothesis about these female figurines is that they do, in fact, represent a fertility goddess. The excavator of Çatal Hüyük, for example, concludes, from the statues found, that the main divinity was "evidently" a goddess,

8

and, further, that this Anatolian goddess was the prototype of the many fertility goddesses known to us in the historical period, such as Hepat, Artemis, Aphrodite and Cybele. It is decisive for him that the statues are found only in shrines.

Another view, however, is that these statuettes had a magical function. They do not represent a goddess but the desired condition of the women who placed them in the shrine. On this understanding they would still relate to fertility and to religion but they would be a type of votive offering rather than cult images. In terms of modern psychology we might call them expressions of wish-fulfillment. The earliest historical religions (Egyptian and Sumerian) provide a sufficient number of parallels to make this hypothesis highly credible.

Who made these figurines? Who, in fact, was responsible for the marvelous paintings at Altamira, Lascaux, Tassili and elsewhere? That is, were they painted by men or by women? I have never seen it suggested that they were done by women, and yet the scholars who take it for granted that they were done by men are the same ones who tell us that in primitive (i.e., pre-historic) society men were off for days on end in hunting parties, leaving their women behind to pass the time as best they could. Indeed one scholar suggests that this accounts for woman's proverbial unpunctuality. But is it not possible that women were the great artists of the pre-historic world? Would not they, for purely biological reasons known best to themselves in an unscientific world, be better prepared than any man to represent how they should look if they were to provide the offspring which were so important? Were not they the ones provided with the leisure to experiment with pictures of the animals they saw as a matter of course and to depict them in terms of the hunting expeditions their absent males talked about? I do not think this is an idle or foolish question because, as we shall see, early historic man endowed woman with an expertise in what we would call the art of civilization, and this must be explained somehow. Why is it, moreover, that the earliest civilized societies in the Mediterranean world were matriarchically structured? Obviously, woman alone was competent to raise children but the young boys must have passed from her control at an early age to join the male hunting pack. Is it not likely that, again because of her leisure time, woman was the recorder and, as such, not only in the best position to recall the immediate past, but also in the only position to know which boys were the offspring of the most successful (i.e., aggressive and victorious) males?

We must, however, return to the original question: Did earliest man think of God as a woman? I think it must be fairly clear that the existence of female figurines, most of them grotesquely obese as noted, does not prove this—does not, in fact, even strongly suggest it since an equally acceptable alternate view is at hand. However, it cannot be gainsaid that in the most ancient historical religions a mother goddess played a leading role. Moreover, the evidence from Çatal Hüyük is more extensive and, although it is just antecedent to the beginnings of recorded history, it must reflect the tradition of earlier generations. On the wall of the most important shrine there is a row of breasts. These are not votive offerings but part of the permanent decoration of the shrine. They call to mind immediately the very much later image of Diana of Ephesus, a figure covered with rows of breasts, thus explaining Professor Mellaart's conviction that the statuettes at Çatal Hüyük are the prototypes of later Mediterranean goddesses—but they must also say something about the religious belief of the people who built this shrine. No one acquainted with primitive man's situation will deny that his basic concern was with reproduction—whether of his own species, before he settled down to an agrarian culture, or of his crops, including livestock thereafter—and consequently this focus on the female organ of nourishment in a religious context suggests that he thought of the divine as

11

he thought (and let us be clear the "he" includes "she") of woman, who both bears new life within her and keeps it alive after birth.

Nevertheless, there is another feature in the Çatal Hüyük shrines which deserves careful attention: the recurrent models of bulls' heads and bulls' horns. Not only are these, like the women's breasts, part of the permanent decoration of the shrine, but they are combined, in striking ways, with the female organs to compose patterns of an essentially unified cult-object. The bull is, of course, a favorite motif in pre-historic and later religious art. He is, also, the symbol *par excellence* of strength and power—a representative of the masculine characteristics necessary for survival in a primitive society. Male human figures appear in pre-historic art but not, it would seem, in any way suggesting divinity. The same cannot be said of the bull figure. The latter, then, represents that aspect of the divine which we would call masculine. What primitive art may really reveal, accordingly, is that pre-historic man did not think of God as either male or female, but as both. It may also—surely we do not even have to guard our words here—reveal his ability to abstract, for the purpose of symbolization, the female breast (not a peculiarity of the human species) and the male horn (which human males early appropriated as a head ornament) representing the totality of all that early man conceived

12

what we call God to be. This suspicion is supported by later evidence, that is, the fact that we find bi-polar gods and goddesses in various ancient mythologies. Bi-polarism in a deity signifies the presence of opposite qualities in his or her character, qualities so opposed as to seem irreconcilable to us. For the ordinary man the most obvious example of this would be someone who was both male and female. This is what we find in very early Mesopotamian texts relating to Ishtar (who is even sometimes represented with a beard) and in the far removed Vedic myths of Siva and Kali. But sex is not the only example of bi-polarism. We find it also in the personalities of gods who are simultaneously healers and destroyers (the Syrian Rešep and the Hellenic Apollo) or lords of life and of death (the Egyptian Osiris).

A much later, and therefore much more guarded, attempt to deal with this can be seen in the legend of Heracles and Omphale. This great model of virility is seduced into interchanging roles with the Lydian queen and allows himself to play the woman's role. Though not born a god, Heracles becomes such in Graeco-Roman religion, and he was, certainly, the most popular object of worship in the ancient pre-Christian Hellenistic world. It is this latter fact which most interests us because the distinction between male and female deities in the classical period was clear-cut; an exception, such as Hermaphroditus, did not represent the canonically sanctioned condition of divine beings. The emergence of sexual ambivalence in a popular hero like Heracles betrays the lingering conviction that the godly is all-encompassing.

Bibliography

E. O. James: *Cult of the Mother-Goddess*, London, 1959.

G. R. Levy: *The Gate of Horn*, London, 1963.

J. Mellaart: *Çatal Hüyük, A Neolithic City in Anatolia*, London, 1965.

S. Moscati (ed.): *Le Antiche Divinità Semitiche*, Rome, 1958.

E. Neumann: *The Great Mother*, Princeton, 1963.

C. Seltman: *Women in Antiquity*, New York, 1962.

II

Whether or not it is quite accurate to state that history begins at Sumer, as the title of one scholarly work affirms, it is certainly true that Sumerian writings are among the oldest produced by man and fall very close to, if not right on, that metaphorical line which separates pre-historic from literate humanity. It is not without interest, then—at least in terms of the previous section—to discover what role "woman" played in the mythological concepts of divinity recorded by the Sumerians. We must not make the mistake, however, of equating the Sumerians with earliest civilized man. It is certain that the Sumerians, a people of some mystery and strange language, entered the Mesopotamian basin not as first settlers but as invaders, or, perhaps, as peaceful immigrants. They seem to have come from the region of the Ural mountains in what is now Soviet Russia, and a number of students of Sumerology think that the Ziggurats (stepped pyramids) they built as temples were substitutes for the mountains they had left behind and, as such, relatively comfortable accommodations for the gods they had brought with them. But there were certainly civilized (though, so far as we know, not literate) people living in the Mesopotamian delta when they arrived. The scholar whose book was mentioned above thinks that these earlier residents may have hurried off to the Indus Valley when the Sumerians arrived and begun a civilization there which was as great as any in the ancient world. It is also certain that whoever began the Indus Valley civilization developed a hieroglyphic form of writing which we, after nearly a century, are still unable to read. There will be great excitement when this script is finally deciphered. In any case, we must suppose some inter-action on the level of religious ideas between the Sumerians and the people they conquered, just as the Israelites, centuries later, were much affected by Canaanite religion, even though officially they repudiated the Canaanite gods.

Among the Sumerian myths which have been miraculously preserved on clay tablets is one dubbed "Inanna and Enki." Enki was one of the three most important gods of Sumer, being principally the lord of all wisdom and the organizer of society for all peoples. He dwelt in the Abzu, the watery deep which was regarded as the womb of creation. His principal temple was at Eridu, the ancient city which purportedly marked the site of the first Sumerian settlement. In his possession were the "mes" of civilization, the rules and regulations governing religious, social and cosmic realities (as, e.g., kingship, truth, art, music, sexual intercourse, descent into and ascent from the nether world, etc.). Inanna, the tutelary goddess of Erech, a prominent divinity of contrasting moods and powers, sets out to secure the "mes" for herself and her city. She takes a pleasant boat ride down to Eridu where she is warmly greeted by Enki who calls her, here, his daughter. Enki commands that a lavish feast be prepared, and he and Inanna sit down to enjoy it. Enki is carried away both by the wine he drinks and the charm of his guest. Nothing is too good for her, and before the feast is over he has given her all the "mes" for which she politely thanks him. She loads them into her boat and sails for home. When Enki sobers up he realizes what he has done and makes a desperate effort to prevent Inanna's "boat of heaven" from reaching Erech. Sea monsters are sent after it and Inanna's journey is interrupted several times. Enki's messenger, Izimud, who meets her along the route, asks for the return of the "mes" but Inanna refuses to hand them over and points out that "her father" is acting most shamefully in going back on his word. Despite further interference from the sea monsters, Inanna arrives safely back in Erech and unloads the "mes" amid great jubilation.

On the face of it this myth is merely a charming story which underscores the very human weaknesses of the Sumerian gods and relates how the "mes" of civilization came to be transferred from Eridu to Erech (Uruk). Like all myths, of course, it attempts to explain something—in this case, presumably, how Erech succeeded Eridu as the center of Mesopotamian civilization. Possibly the myth was created as a piece of what we would call propaganda, though it may simply reflect the actual passage of cultural influence from one city to another and, on that score, might have originated in Eridu as easily as in Erech. The excavations carried out at Erech in the fifties have, as a matter of fact, shown that it must be regarded as the "keystone" of Mesopotamian archaeology. Inasmuch as Inanna was the tutelary deity of Erech (as Enki was tutelary god of Eridu), we should naturally expect her, in this myth, to be the cause of Erech's success in appropriating the prestige of Eridu, but we must not forget that these people took their gods and goddesses seriously—human-like frailties notwithstanding— and, accordingly, the myth at least suggests that only she was capable of carrying out this coup. It further suggests that civilization was under her patronage and that only she was interested enough in it to obtain its constituent elements from the god who had created them. Inanna was one of the seven principal deities in the Sumerian pantheon, but not the foremost of the seven nor even the only female among them—she shared that distinction with Ninhursag, the great mother goddess who was probably the consort of An, the chief, though largely otiose god, from whom the others descended. As often happens in polytheistic pantheons, we find a younger generation of gods superseding the older, and this happened in Mesopotamia where Enlil and Inanna (Marduk and Ishtar in Babylonian times) rise to greater prominence than An and Ninhursag.

This view of Inanna as the patroness of civilization—and this necessarily says something about her sex—is supported by that episode in the Gilgamesh epic which tells how Enkidu was civilized. Gilgamesh was the most famous of the kings of Erech (Uruk) but overbearing and arrogant. In answer to the pleadings of the subjects of the great king, the gods created Enkidu who might match Gilgamesh in strength and determination. But Enkidu represented unspoiled human nature, i.e., uncivilized. He was literature's first Tarzan, its first "noble savage," and he lived, unclothed, with the beasts of the forest. In order for him to be "tamed," to come in contact with the haughty lord of Uruk, he had to learn the basics of civilization. To this end a temple prostitute, a representative of Ishtar (Inanna), is brought out to the watering hole where Enkidu drinks. She exposes her charms to Enkidu and he succumbs to them for "six days and seven nights."

19

At the end of that time the prostitute (one must not think of her as engaging in something shameful—this was a religious profession for those who entered it) advises him: "You are wise, Enkidu, and now you have become like a god." Enkidu seeks out again his former companions of the forest, the wild beasts, but they will no longer come near him. He has indeed been changed, but how? Through intercourse with a woman. Is this a blessing or a curse? This question does not concern the story-tellers responsible for the epic as we have it; they are content to let us know by what means it was possible for Enkidu to enter civilized society. Of course, that says a great deal by itself and surely intimates the belief that woman civilizes.

The same idea reappears in other ancient literature but with a more pronounced bias—if indeed we can speak at all of a bias in the epic of Gilgamesh. In the book of Genesis, Adam and Eve are forbidden to eat of the tree of the knowledge of good and evil (a phrase that signifies *all* knowledge). The serpent—a symbolic figure which we shall not here attempt to analyze—tells Eve that if she and Adam eat of the tree they will become as gods (Gen 3, 5) and that this is why the Lord has forbidden them to partake of its fruit. Eve is tempted, to the point of yielding, but why? Because she sees that "the tree was desirable for the purpose of knowing" (Gen 3, 6).

We all know the consequences of Eve's seduction according to the biblical narrative, but it is of great interest for us to note that, like Inanna, she cares about knowledge. It is she whom the enigmatic serpent approaches, thereby implying that she would be more readily tempted by the promise of wisdom than her male spouse. Eve, in turn, seduces Adam, and indeed, like Enkidu, he is no longer an innocent thereafter, though the biblical narrator clearly depicts this as a fall from grace.

In the Greek myth of Pandora we have another version of this tale. Prometheus, one of the Titans but a lesser god in terms of developed Greek mythology, risks his status to bring fire—and, through it, civilization—to man. For this he is punished by Zeus. Moreover, in order to offset the benefits given to mankind by Prometheus, Zeus has the gods fashion an irresistibly beautiful and accomplished woman, Pandora, who is bestowed on Epimetheus as a wife. She brings with her a box (really a jar) containing all the evils and miseries which could afflict man. When Epimetheus opens this box the varieties of pestilence fly out and descend upon mankind. Hesiod, who is our earliest authority for this story, concludes it by saying: "This was the origin of the damnable race of women—a plague which men must live with." What we seem to have here in these three myths is a gradual inversion of the role of woman. In the earliest, she is an agent of civilization—though even there she is indirectly responsible for man's (Enkidu's) loss of rapport with the animal world. In Genesis, she is over-eager for wisdom and disobeys the divine command, thus losing both innocence and immortality for herself and her descendants. In Hesiod, she is no longer associated with knowledge but altogether with misfortune, of which she is the agent for all men. Historically, the change is from matrilinear and matriarchal society to one that is patrilinear and patriarchal. Perhaps the very earliest indication of this inversion is discernible in our myth of Inanna and Enki, for it is by taking advantage of her father's inebriation and delight in her company that the goddess wrests the all-important "mes" from him.

I do not think it is absurd to surmise that, once man had settled down to an agricultural type of community, he (and here I mean the male) took over those pastimes which had previously been the preserve of his women-folk. Surely some substitute had to be found for the hunt that was no longer essential and some outlet for the energy that had gone into it. But he also had to be without rival in this as he had been in killing the boar, the stag, and the lion. Any indication that woman had been pre-eminent in the domain which now mattered (art and reflection) had to be at least veiled. But the veil is fairly transparent inasmuch as we are able to see through it in the myths that survive. Even in the myth of Pandora it is not wholly opaque. The decision of Zeus to unleash Pandora on humanity was prompted by Prometheus' previous communication of the fundamentals of civilization. Prometheus, in turn, had been taught all art and knowledge by Athena so that, even in this tradition, knowledge had come to man, albeit indirectly, through a woman.

In terms of understanding the process which I have referred to as the "inversion" of the woman's role, the myths surrounding Athena and the actual historical evolution of the goddess are particularly instructive. As Athena, she is the goddess of the city of Athens and there is no doubt that she was originally a Minoan house-goddess with her shrine in the royal palace. In this respect she belongs to a matrilinear and matriarchal cultural milieu. The Dorian Greeks brought with them from the north a warrior goddess, Pallas (a Palladion is a combination of two thunder shields, set one above the other like a figure 8). The two goddesses are combined, with Pallas emerging as the dominant personality. The old Minoan-Mycenaen goddess recedes into the background except for her name and her snake and bird companions. Pallas is the creature of a society which has already become patriarchal in structure. She is scarcely a woman, and Gilbert

Murray rightly refers to her as a "sexless Valkyrie." The wonder is that the Dorians held a female divinity in esteem at all. The old fears and prejudices seem to have been exorcised by what J. E. Harrison calls "the outrageous myth" of the birth of Athena from the head of Zeus. Here we see the male determination to suppress any female domination. Athena (not the Minoan goddess, of course) is actually conceived in the womb of Metis, a goddess who is herself Prudence. Zeus is the father, but when he learns that the wise mother is about to bear a child who might be even more intelligent than herself— and certainly more so than him—he devours her. The child is born, however, but from her father's head, and she emerges fully clad in armor. As Miss Harrison puts it, she is turned into a "diagram of motherless birth." Nevertheless, we can see that all of this is but a camouflage for the fact that Athena is predominantly a goddess of wisdom. This is the prerogative of her sex, and though she is virtually sexless and even born from a paternal head rather than from a maternal womb, she remains a woman, the virgin of Athens. The myth-making barely conceals the frantic effort to put womankind in her place while grudgingly admitting her gifts of the mind.

Bibliography

J. E. Bruns: "Old Testament History and the
Development of a Sexual Ethic," in *The New
Morality*, New York, 1967.

J. E. Harrison: *Themis*, New York, 1962 (first
published 1912).

S. N. Kramer: *Sumerian Mythology*, New York,
1961 (first published 1944).

————: *History Begins at Sumer*, New York,
1956.

————: *The Sumerians*, Chicago, 1963.

G. Murray: *Five Stages of Greek Religion*, New
York, 1955.

M. P. Nilsson: *A History of Greek Religion*,
New York, 1964.

III

The other ancient civilization rivaling Meso-potamia's in the claim to be the first which is historical is that of Egypt, and if we are to grant the Sumero-Babylonian Inanna-Ishtar a chrono-logical precedence which perhaps she does not deserve, we cannot ascribe to her the same lon-gevity and vitality shown by the great Egyptian goddess Isis. Of all the goddesses of antiquity, none achieved the fame and popularity of Isis.

Egyptian mythology is very complex and does not lend itself to orderly systematization. The Greeks attempted to harmonize it but were not really successful. Part of the reason for the dif-ferences that we find in the Egyptian myths about the gods is that there were two great centers of priestly activity in ancient Egypt (to say nothing of minor centers), one in the north at Heliopolis (the biblical On) and the other in the south at Thebes. It was natural that the distance between these sites (nearly five hundred miles) would lead to variations in the telling of stories about the gods. Moreover, like most ancient writers, the

Egyptians were more interested in including everything that had been handed down by oral or written tradition than in eliminating disparate material for the sake of coherence. Finally, there is discernible a process of evolution in the mythology reflecting both social changes and expanding religious awareness. All of these factors combine to make a single account of any one of the gods impossible. Nevertheless, the main outlines of the story and character of Isis stand out clearly against the multitude of conflicting details.

The goddess appears as the sister and wife of Osiris. She and her brother, together with another brother-sister pair, Seth and Nephthys, belonged to the fourth generation of gods, descending from Ra. Osiris was the primeval king and benefactor of mankind. Through treachery he is murdered by his jealous brother Seth, who sets his dismembered corpse adrift in a box. Isis and Nephthys, overcome with sorrow, go off in search of the body of Osiris which they recover. Isis resuscitates the dead Osiris and impregnates herself with his seed. Though alive, Osiris does not return to an earthly life but becomes lord of the underworld and judge of the dead. Isis bears him a son, Horus, whom she rears in secret to protect him from Seth. In time, Horus avenges his father and assumes his regal power.

From this very brief sketch it must be apparent that Isis represents the dutiful and loving wife and mother. These are her outstanding qualities and in terms of popular appeal they account, by themselves, for the attraction she had for worshipers. But there is more to Isis than this. She was known as "the great enchantress" and magical incantations were invariably ascribed to her. Her ability to revive Osiris is an indication of this power. How did she come by it? Interestingly enough, the explanation of this is not unlike the myth about Inanna and Enki already outlined. Isis wished to know the secret name of Ra. Common to all ancient peoples is the notion that the name expresses the nature of the person who bears it. To know someone's name is to exercise a kind of power over that person (if one reflects on it, this notion is not far-fetched even today). To know the secret name of a god, known only to himself, is to acquire his power. Ra, of course, was unwilling to divulge his secret name, but Isis formed a serpent from a handful of earth and spittle that had dropped from the mouth of Ra. She endowed the serpent with an excruciatingly painful and venomous bite and placed it in a position to strike at Ra as the god began his daily procession of state. Once bitten, the god cried out for assistance from his descendants, the younger gods and goddesses. Only Isis promised to cure the pain, but on condition that Ra tell her his secret name. At first the god demurred, reciting the names which everyone knew, but when he found that he could no longer walk, he declared: "I consent that Isis shall search into me and that my name shall pass from me into her." And so it happened that Isis alone possessed all the knowledge of the creator-god.

Equally interesting is the significance attached by Isis herself, in a hymn of the Middle Kingdom, to the impregnation she was able to effect. Though revived, Osiris was inert and his male member flaccid. According to one version of the myth, the phallus was never even found, since it had been swallowed by a fish when Seth threw the dismembered body into the waters. Isis, however, is able to draw semen from her husband, and in view of this she exclaims: "There is no god who has done what I have done, nor a goddess: I made myself to a man, though I was a woman."

My point in selecting these two incidents in the Isis story is, of course, to underline the fact that she achieved, by her own efforts, equal status with the two principal male gods of ancient Egypt: Ra and Osiris. But we must remember that Isis is a product of man's religious intuition and that, accordingly, what she does, or what happens to her, in the ancient myths is really an expression of what was happening in human consciousness. The conclusion might well be drawn that in Egypt, as in Mesopotamia, the myth-makers—which means the spokesmen for the people—understood that the highest prerogatives of divinity were not restricted to one sex.

On the other hand it would be foolish to maintain that this was a fully conscious awareness. It should rather be seen as a sub-conscious development and as a dim recollection of the time when the idea of "god" did not focus on one sex as distinguished from the other. The very name of Isis would help to rescue such archetypal symbols from conscious oblivion. In Egyptian, the hieroglyph for her name is a throne. We have only an approximate idea of how the ancient Egyptians pronounced their words, but this one probably sounded something like *ašet*. In most representations of Isis she wears the throne on her head, emphasizing the correspondence between name and function. What function is this? It is a very ancient, pre-historic one, according to the best authorities. The great mother goddess of pre-historic man (or, in view of what we have seen, the aspect of the divine which we call goddess) is symbolized not only by her breasts, or her distended abdomen and buttocks, but also by her broad expanse of thigh, her lap, on which the newborn child can sit, as if enthroned. Anthropologists see in the very ancient concepts of throne and "accession" to the throne a carry-over from the more primitive (pre-historic) experience of gaining power and, indeed, sustenance from the mother. In other words, the throne, as such, is a symbol of the mother and, even when this had been forgotten, a symbol of male dependence upon the woman not just for life but also for power. Understanding this, we can appreciate how close a link Isis is to the pre-historic era. In the mythology surrounding her we see, of course, how she literally fulfills her function by nurturing the infant Horus, and the most frequently discovered figurines of Isis—they number in the thousands—are precisely those in which she holds her young son on her lap.

Bibliography

C. J. Bleeker: "Isis as Saviour Goddess," in *The Saviour God* (E. O. James Festschrift), Manchester & New York, 1963.

R. T. Rundle Clark: *Myth and Symbol in Ancient Egypt,* New York, 1960.

R. E. Witt: *Isis in the Graeco-Roman World,* Ithaca, 1971.

Part Two

The World of the Bible

I

There is nothing in the Hebrew Scriptures to suggest that Yahweh was ever considered as other than utterly masculine by his worshipers. Is this true? The image of a strong, protective and sometimes wrathful patriarch seems to stare at us from every page, whether it is when saying of David, "I will be a father to him, and he shall be a son to me. And if he does wrong, I will correct him with the rod of men" (2 Sam 7, 14), or to Israel, "Again I passed by you and saw that you were now old enough for love. So I spread the corner of my cloak over you to cover your nakedness" (Ezek 16, 8), or when he is seen by the prophet Isaiah as a king "seated on a high and lofty throne, with the train of his garment filling the temple" (Is 6, 1). He is the Lord, whose angry voice rumbles forth from his mouth (Job 37, 2), the God of hosts, leader of the armies of Israel (2 Sam 17, 45), the rider of the cherubim who forges his arrows and scatters them (Ps 18, 11. 15). In the midst of so much that is distinctively masculine, there seems little likelihood of finding a trace of the opposite sex. But it is there. It is there, first of all, in the creation account: "God said, 'Let us make mankind in our image and likeness.' God created man in his image. In the image of God he created him. Male and female he created them."

We are so accustomed to thinking that "image and likeness" here means "with intelligence and freedom" or something of that sort that we do not pause to consider what the Hebrew writer himself meant. The outstanding modern commentator on Genesis (G. Von Rad) notes that the Hebrew wording here must include man's bodily appearance, and he warns against splitting the physical from the spiritual: "The whole man is created in God's image." This being so, it is difficult to see how we can avoid the conclusion that Yahweh is both male and female. This is certainly not something emphasized in the Bible, but it is in accordance with the ancient view of divinity as bi-polar, of which we have seen other examples.

It is there, secondly, in the numerous passages scattered throughout the sapiential books in which wisdom is personified (Prv 8, 1—9, 12; 1, 20-33; 3, 13-18; 4, 7-9; Wis 6, 12—11, 1; Sir 1, 1-18; 4, 11-19; 24, 1-21; Bar 3, 15-38). The wisdom in question here is, of course, the wisdom of God, a divine attribute but spoken of as having an independent existence. Now the word for wisdom in Hebrew *(hôkmah)* is feminine gender, and this partly explains the remarkable fact that divine wisdom as personified in these writings is a woman. But scholars are not generally satisfied that this lexical accident accounts for the more specific features of this intriguing figure: her cosmic search and journey (Sir 24, 3-7), her playing as a child before the Lord (Prv 8, 30), her "I" style of speech and the constant association made between herself and life and prosperity. These are all very reminiscent of the descriptions of the Egyptian goddess Maat on the one hand and of the so-called Isis aretalogies on the other. Whether this biblical characterization of wisdom first appeared before or after the exile (the passages in Proverbs are the oldest, but just how old is disputed) does not affect the genuine possibility of an influence from Egyptian sources. Of course, this is not to suggest that the biblical writers were equating divine wisdom with one or another foreign deity, but that they found it useful to speak of wisdom in terms borrowed from the familiar mythology and literature of Egypt. Of interest to us is the stronger emphasis this places on the sex of wisdom, making it clear that our authors were not embarrassed by the grammatical necessity of referring to divine wisdom as female, but found it suitable enough to warrant the kind of development requiring their appropriation of elements native to other religious literature.

Are we confronted here, then, in these texts from the Old Testament with a further instance of the concept that knowledge is a feminine gift? Our earlier study showed that the desire for knowledge was—in the biblical narrative—a feminine trait (Eve's), but also it was represented there as evil. These later passages seem to reflect a stage in the evolution of Israelite religion when patriarchy was established firmly enough to allow for the reappearance of the very ancient conviction that wisdom and woman were inseparable, and that, furthermore, wisdom was not inimical to man but, on the contrary, his guarantee of "the good life" whether in the judgment of God or in that of his fellow human beings. Since our knowledge of the many factors which shaped the course of Yahwism is limited and, for the period in question, largely hypothetical, we can only surmise, but it does seem to be true in the history of religions that earlier beliefs submerged or driven underground by other concerns reappear at a later date. We can see this clearly in the Indian religions, whether Hindu or Buddhist. The Vedic gods of the conquering Aryans are gradually superseded by older, Dravidian gods: Šiva, who has no role to play in the early hymns, is certainly the *Mahayogi* and *Pašupati* of the Indus

Valley Seals, and the gods of Hinduism—reduced
to total irrelevance by Gotama—find their way
back into later (Mahayana) Buddhism as Bod-
hisattvas (Maitreya, the Buddha to come, is the
old Indo-Aryan god Mithra),

Of course, divine wisdom is not another god
(dess) than Yahweh. She is, as said above, simply Yahweh considered under one rubric, but the
very fact that this "consideration" occurs at all is
remarkable. Early Christian writers saw in this
personification a foreshadowing of the doctrine
of the Trinity. Divine wisdom was none other
than the Word of God, the second person of the
Trinity (the Word of God and his wisdom are
equated in Wis 9, 1). We may view it, conversely,
as the resurrection of the very ancient idea that
the divine is all things.

Having mentioned the Christian interpretation of these passages in the first centuries of our
era, we might well point out another aspect of
Yahweh which, though frequently mentioned in
the Old Testament, is never developed along the
personal lines given to his wisdom: his Spirit.
Like wisdom (*hôkmah*), spirit (*ruah*) in Hebrew
is feminine. The fact that the Spirit of Yahweh is
given great prominence in the Old Testament
(see, e.g., Gen 1, 2; Is 11, 2: Jl 3, 1-2) led the
early Church Fathers to see here a further example
of Trinitarian teaching. In the Greek Scriptures
which the Church used, spirit (*pneuma*) is a

neuter noun, sexless, and this suited the requisites of theological speculation (male-oriented as it was). The Father is obviously masculine, the Word (*Logos* in Greek, also masculine in gender) whom he begets is masculine, and the Spirit which they beget together is neuter. But it is interesting to ponder the course of theological development if the original Hebrew writings had been familiar to the theologians. We have one suggestive indication of what might have happened in a fragment from the lost "Gospel according to the Hebrews." In it, according to the great exegete Origen, Jesus says: "Even now did my mother the Holy Spirit take me by one of my hairs and carry me away to the great mountain Thabor." It is perhaps a tragedy that this concept of the Spirit as feminine was neglected. There is no more reason for Jews or Christians to think of God as masculine (I mean independently of the purely literary and cultural influences which determined the kind of terminology used in our Scriptures) than as feminine. These two examples taken from the same Scriptures indicate that we have ample justification, if we choose, to speak of God as a woman as well as a man.

Bibliography

W. L. Knox: "The Divine Wisdom," *JTS* 38
(1937) pp. 230-237.
C. Kayatz: *Studien zu Proverbien 1-9*, Neukir-
chen-Vluyn, 1966.
R. N. Whybray: *Wisdom in Proverbs*, London,
1965.

II

The imposing masculine image of the God of Israel remains despite the interesting characterization of divine wisdom as feminine. It would be a mistake to conclude from this, however, that woman, as such, plays no religious role in the Old Testament. Sometimes a woman represents the forces opposed to Yahweh, as is the case with Jezebel, whose name has come down to us as the epitome of the evil wanton (cf. 1 Kgs 16, 31— 2 Kgs 9, 37), and with Athaliah (2 Kgs 8, 26; 11, 1-21), one of two women to rule over the nation in her own name (the other was Queen Alexandra Salome just before the beginning of the Christian era); but more often a woman appears as Yahweh's instrument for the furtherance of his designs, and not just in a passive way by becoming, for example, the mother of one of the patriarchs or heroes. (Sarah's giving birth to Isaac is crucial to "salvation history," but she didn't even believe it could come to pass—Gen 18, 9-15. Ruth becomes an ancestress of David, and it might be said that her history teaches that God is not a

egy). Two women, consequently, are celebrated for having gained a crucial victory for Israel. The importance of this victory is assured by the great antiquity of the canticle which celebrates it. Is it not significant that as Israel's entrance into "the promised land" was accomplished through a woman (Rahab), its permanence in that land was guaranteed by two others—women, moreover, who displayed both heroism and intelligence?

We know very little about our next heroine because only a few verses of the second book of Kings speak of her (2 Kgs 11, 1-3), but she preserved almost single-handedly (at least the initiative was hers) the Davidic dynasty. Consequently, in both Jewish and Christian belief, she was God's guarantor of the birth of the Messiah. Jehosheba, for that was her name, figures in a puzzling series of events that took place in Jerusalem in the middle of the ninth century B.C. According to the very sketchy accounts we have (2 Kgs 9, 27-29; 11, 1-20 and parallels in 2 Chr 22, 1—23, 21), when Ahaziah, the king of Judah, was slain, his mother Athaliah, the daughter of Ahab king of Israel (and of his infamous wife Jezebel), took up the reins of power. At the same time, we are told, "she proceeded to kill off all the royal offspring of the house of Judah." Was she thinking of remarrying and founding a new dynasty? It would be easy to suppose that she intended to make one of her brother's children her heir, but all the male descendants of Ahab were put to death at the same time that her son Ahaziah was slain (2 Kgs 10, 1-11). It is difficult to fathom her aim. Perhaps she had some secret agreement with one of the neighboring powers, but although she ruled for six full years her ultimate plans were never realized and they were frustrated by another woman, her stepdaughter. Jehosheba took the infant son of her half-brother Ahaziah "and spirited him away, along with his nurse, from the bedroom where the princes were about to be slain." This, of course, was at the beginning of Athaliah's reign. The child was kept hidden for six years in the private rooms of the temple. Jehosheba is said to have been married to Jehoiada the high priest (2 Chr 22, 11), which may only be the guess of a later writer, but certainly Jehoiada cooperated with the courageous princess, and when the boy was seven, the priest entered into a conspiracy with the captains of the guard to restore the royal line in the person of the young Joash. The carefully arranged plan succeeded and Athaliah was cut down in the street as her grandson was being anointed king in the temple. What dramatic material there is in this episode! It is all the more intriguing because we have only an outline of what happened and so many guesses as to what it may really have been all about. I do not think it impossible that Jehosheba made off with the infant Joash, not because she thought he would be put to death but because she had every reason to believe that her stepmother would bring him up in the Tyrian (Sidonian) worship of Baal. Whatever the reason, Jehosheba displayed great courage and determination, and these were qualities that she had to exercise for six years. She is really one of the unsung heroines of the Old Testament. In our sophistication, we are no longer partisan to the kind of religious conviction which demands this sort of risk (though many of today's young people seem willing to take it for socio-political reasons), but we cannot fail to respect the single-mindedness of Jehosheba. As indicated earlier, her actions were highly significant for believing Jews and Christians.

Three women of the Old Testament have had books named after them. One of them, Ruth, we have already mentioned. The other two, Judith and Esther, belong not only to a much later period but, in all probability, to the realm of fiction. Scholars have delved deeply into the purportedly historical backgrounds of these books but have not been able to correlate the main characters and incidents with known facts. The present, prevailing view is that these books are not history but what we would call historical fiction, and indeed there is no reason why we should not be able to read them as just that. At the same time, we must recognize that historical fiction is not pure fantasy. It emerges from real-life situations, and very often includes real-life personalities.

Judith is a beautiful young widow in the town of Bethulia (unidentified—the name suggests "Virgin of Yahweh" and may point to Jerusalem, although the latter is mentioned frequently in the text and as distant from Bethulia; on the other hand, see Jdt 9, 1-2), which is under siege by the armies of Nebuchadnezzar, king of the Assyrians (the king is real enough, but he never ruled over Assyria which had disappeared from history by his time). As the story goes—too well known to need retelling here—nothing is able to impede the ruthless progress of Holofernes, the principal general of Nebuchadnezzar (the Holofernes of history was a general in the army of Artaxerxes III of Persia), and the Jewish nation, including of course the temple in Jerusalem, is threatened with imminent destruction. Holofernes is encamped outside Bethulia and the local authorities are paralyzed into inaction by fear. Judith has her own plan. Fortified by prayer and the courage of her conviction, she manages to have herself introduced to Holofernes, feigning a desire to betray her own people in order to save herself. But she knows that it is her beauty rather than anything she might have to say which will interest Holofernes. Of course she is right, and she is invited to have supper with him and to spend the night in his tent. Making sure that he has a great deal to drink, Judith bides her time until he falls asleep in a stupor. Then with two quick blows she cuts off his head, puts it into her food basket (the modern shopping bag!) and makes her way back to Bethulia. The invading army is, of course, thrown into consternation and beats a hasty retreat. Judith is the heroine of the day: "You are the glory of Jerusalem, the surpassing joy of Israel; you are the splendid boast of our people" (Jdt 15, 9).

There does not appear to have been any actual event corresponding to the story told in the book of Judith. The tale is viewed as a kind of parable which teaches that the Lord protects his people. In the book of Samuel, the mighty Goliath is defeated by David the stripling. Here a woman defeats another kind of Goliath. But David is certainly the Lord's chosen instrument and so is Judith (even if she is only a fictional character). Her name means, simply, the Jewess, and perhaps she is a female personification of her nation. The prophets often spoke of Israel as the bride of Yahweh and that may be the connotation intended here.

It has been suggested, though not in recent years, that Judith may be a romanticized portrait of Queen Alexandra Salome to whom reference was made earlier. This is an attractive hypothesis and has in its favor the fact that this queen was faced during her reign with the threat of an invasion by the armies of Tigranes of Armenia. The threat did not materialize because domestic troubles in Armenia forced the return of the king's army (cf. Josephus: *Antiquities* XIII, 16), but we can well imagine this sort of book being written at the time when the peril was real, especially since the queen had the respect and support of her people. What Josephus writes of her could be said of Judith: "A woman she was who showed no signs of the weakness of her sex, for she was sagacious to the greatest degree." However, there are serious reasons for thinking that the book of Judith, in one form or another, antedated the reign of Queen Alexandra Salome (76-69 B.C.), but this does not in any way diminish the significance of Judith as a symbol of "woman—the right hand of God."

If Judith comes close to resembling an actual personality of note, Esther does not. There are good reasons (disputed, of course) for thinking that Esther is the same individual as the Scheherazade of Persian legend—a name made famous by the beautiful music of Rimsky-Korsakoff—and equally as fictional. We know too much about Persian history at this period (somewhere between 486 and 465 B.C., the reign of Xerxes I) to be able to credit the author of the book of Esther with any accuracy. Like the author of Judith, he is not interested in history as such but in an idea: the idea that Yahweh, in strange and wondrous ways, protects his people. This is, of course, the very same theme underlying the book of Judith, and it has, not surprisingly, been suggested that both books were composed in the second century B.C. to serve the same purpose: to encourage the Jews at a time when their national identity was being threatened by the dead-weight of Seleucid (Greek) rule in the Near and Middle East.

Esther's uncle and guardian, the Jew Mordecai, had at one time foiled a plot on the life of King Ahasuerus (Xerxes). The conspirators who were put to death had been cronies of Haman, the prime minister. Haman, so the story goes, took himself very seriously and expected all the king's subjects to bend the knee to him. Mordecai, however, would not do this, and this enraged Haman who thereupon determined to rid the realm not only of Mordecai but of all of Mordecai's troublesome fellow Jews. He accordingly set a date for a massive pogrom which is approved by the king (who does not know that Mordecai and his other Jewish subjects are to be the victims—one of the many indications in the narrative that our author is not dealing with facts). In the meanwhile the king has changed wives. Vashti, the queen, refused to obey his command to present herself to his nobles on the occasion of a great celebration and was forthwith deprived of her royal status. All the beautiful young maid-

51

ens of the empire were then brought together to be prepared for presentation to the king. From among them he would choose the one most pleasing to him and she would become queen. The choice fell on Esther, the niece of Mordecai. The denouement of the tale is predictable. Esther, risking her position at court, tells the king what Haman had planned to do and that her uncle, who had once saved the king's life, was the primary object of Haman's murderous intentions. Of course, Esther's intervention is successful and Haman is hanged on the day he had set for the slaughter of the Jews. The author of this book then assures us that, with the king's permission, the Jews put to death seventy-five thousand of their foes, and from that time the 13th and 14th of Adar have been celebrated by Jews everywhere as the feast of Purim (Adar extends roughly from mid-February to mid-March). The name of the feast is supposed to derive from the word *pûr* (lot)—Haman had cast lots to determine the date on which he should put his plan into execution, the day that turned out to be fatal for him. However, it is generally thought that this is a contrived explanation for the meaning of the word "purim" and that we do not really know how the festival came to be called by this name.

Is there some special significance to the fact that these two heroines, Judith and Esther, are fictional? Prior to them or, rather, to their appearance in literature, the last heroes of the Old Testament are Nehemiah and Ezra, and after their appearance only Judas Maccabeus and his brothers achieve heroic stature. These remarkable women belong to that period in the history of Israel when little happened or, at least, seems to have happened because we have no record of it. The two hundred years between the end of the fifth century B.C. and the end of the third are marked chiefly by Israel's passing from subordination to Persian rule to that of the Greeks. It appears to have been a period of disillusionment for the Jews without any prospect of a change in their fortunes. It is a period rather well reflected in the book of Ecclesiastes or Qoheleth in which the author bears witness to the monotony of existence: "What has happened will happen again, and what has been done will be done again, and there is nothing new under the sun" (Eccl 1, 9). Israel is far now from both the triumph of conquest and the humiliation of exile. And because she seemed no longer to have any destiny, her God appeared to have grown remote and inaccessible: "God is in heaven, you are on earth; so let your words be few" (Eccl 5, 2). It was probably earlier in this same period that the book of Job was written, and because it was earlier it reflects more anguish about this withdrawal of God: "He destroys blameless and wicked alike. When a sudden flood brings death he mocks the plight of the innocent" (Jb 9, 22-23). Time and again the author of Job accuses God of indifference.

One certain result of this "silence" of God was the development of popular interest in angels, charmingly illustrated in the book of Tobit. If Yahweh is distant and unapproachable, his angels are not, and they become the ordinary man's helpers and advocates: "When you and Sarah prayed, it was I who brought your prayers into the glorious presence of the Lord" (Tb 12, 12).

Another consequence was the personification of divine wisdom to which we have already given some attention. We noticed that wisdom is described as engaged in a cosmic search and journey. She also takes on the role of a street preacher, an evangelist: "Wisdom cries aloud in the streets, she raises her voice in public places; she calls in the market place and proclaims at the open gates of the city" (Prv 1, 20-21); she appears on earth and lives among men (Bar 3, 47) and, in fact, she becomes tangible in the Torah (Bar 4, 1; Sir 24, 23).

Our heroines, Judith and Esther, who are children of this same period, are like the angels and the divine wisdom, the products of religious imagination, but they also seem to serve the same function: to substitute for God himself. In the distant past Yahweh had struck down the enemies of his people; Yahweh had spoken to Moses and

54

the prophets; Yahweh had given the commandments on Sinai. Now it is the angels who communicate with man; it is divine wisdom which teaches man, and it is two idealized heroines who defeat the foes of Israel. Looked at in this way, our heroines really take on a quasi-divine character. We should be very wary of suggesting this if they belonged to another period of Israelite history, but as it is they share enough traits with the other idealizations of their period to warrant at least the suggestion.

III

The New Testament presents itself as the fulfillment of the Old. The Messiah, the Son of God promised by the prophets and psalmists, has come. In its pages Jesus is also shown to be the incarnate word and wisdom of God (especially in the prologues to the gospel and first letter of John), the very glory or presence of God which the Jews called *kabôd* or *shekinah* (Hebrews 1, 3; James 2, 1). In the books of the Old Testament the *shekinah,* visualized as a luminous cloud, descends upon the tent of meeting and, later, the Temple of Solomon (Ex 40, 34-35; 1 Kgs 8, 10-13; Ez 10, 2-4). In the New Testament the *shekinah* descends upon Mary, the mother of Jesus (Lk 2, 35), thereby signifying that the presence of God literally rested within her as she carried her child in the womb. This theme is continued in Luke's infancy narrative through the parallelisms made there between Mary and the ark: Elizabeth wonders how the mother of her Lord should come to her as David wonders how the ark of the Lord should come to him

(2 Sam 6, 9). Mary stays with Elizabeth for three
months, just as the ark remained in the house of
Obed-edom, where David had directed it to be
placed, for three months (2 Sam 6, 11). The
theme reappears in the last book of the New
Testament, the Apocalypse or Revelation of John.
After the seventh angel has blown his trumpet,
"God's temple in heaven was opened and the ark
of his covenant was seen within his temple . . .
and a great portent appeared in heaven, a woman
clothed with the sun, with the moon under her
feet, and on her head a crown of twelve stars;
she was with child and she cried out in her pangs
of birth, in anguish for delivery" (Apoc 11, 19
—12, 2). The woman here is a complex symbol.
She is the Church, surely, for "the rest of her
offspring" are those "who keep the commandments of God and bear testimony to Jesus"
(Apoc 12, 17) but she is also clearly the mother
of Jesus, for the child she brings forth here is "a
male child who is to rule all the nations with a
rod of iron" (Apoc 12, 5; cf. Ps 2, 9). Accordingly she appears here first in this passage as the
ark of the covenant, the seat of the divine presence. The ark was indeed regarded as a throne
(1 Chr 28, 2-18) but ostensibly empty since
Yahweh "no man may see and live" (Ex 33, 20).
Only the cloud of the presence, the *shekinah,*
might be seen to rest upon it. But the ark of the

new covenant is a mother whose child is the now visible glory of God: "And going into the house they saw the child with Mary his mother, and they fell down and worshiped him" (Mt 2, 11).

In the next section of this little study we will have to consider Mary under a number of other aspects, but this initial view of her as the throne of the Lord is taken directly from the New Testament and, as the reader will recognize, it clearly relates the mother of Jesus to one of the most ancient symbols of the mother goddess and, ironically, to the Isis whom she was eventually to supplant in the shrines of the Mediterranean world. There is no implication here that Mary is represented as a goddess in any part of the New Testament, but I am saying that this particular aspect of her marks the beginning, and an auspicious one, of theological reflections about her which lead to assigning her a status just short of the divine.

Let us conclude these remarks with part of an invocation to Mary composed by Germanus, patriarch of Constantinople in the eighth century, keeping in mind how easily it might have been written by an Egyptian priest of Isis in the century before the Christian era: "You will be called the throne bearing God, and the Royal Chair of the King of Heaven, for you are Queen and Sovereign Lady."

Bibliography

R. Laurentin: *Queen of Heaven,* London and
Dublin, 1956.

Part Three

The Christian and Modern World

I

Apart from the infancy gospels the mother of Jesus does not figure very largely in the New Testament. In the fourth gospel she appears twice, at the beginning and at the end of her son's public ministry. It is she who asks Jesus to come to the assistance of their embarrassed hosts at Cana (Jn 2, 1-11) and it is to her and to the beloved disciple that Jesus, from the cross, addresses the words: "Woman, behold thy Son; Son, behold thy mother" (Jn 19, 26-27). Many exegetes see the way John presents Mary in these two instances as an attempt to cast her in a symbolic role in which she stands for the Church. The disciples of Jesus are entrusted to her and she is given care of them. This corresponds, of course, with the picture of the woman in the twelfth chapter of the Apocalypse who, it will be remembered, is both the mother of Jesus and the mother of "those who keep the commandments of God and bear testimony to Jesus" (Apoc 12, 17). The concept of Mary as mother of all those who have life in the name of Jesus calls to mind that other woman who was called "the mother of all the living" (Gen 3, 20), Eve. The parallelism is probably intended, though it is not made explicit by the fourth evangelist. It was, however, soon to be taken up, as we shall see.

In the Acts of the Apostles, Mary appears on the scene in the midst of the earliest Christian community as it awaits the descent of the Holy Spirit on Pentecost, the event that Luke establishes as the birth date of the Church. Her presence for this period may be another example of the symbolic value already attached to her person by the writers of the New Testament (cf. Acts 1, 12—2, 4).

In the letters of Paul, the mother of Jesus is mentioned only once and in the most offhand way (Gal 4, 4), though it is possible that he (or whoever is responsible for the pastoral epistles) alludes to her in 1 Tim 2, 15 (a text which perhaps should be translated "yet woman will be saved by *the* parturition"—i.e., by the fact that Mary gave birth to the Savior). In any case there is certainly an allusion to Genesis 3, 16 here, and if the reading given above is accepted, then to the Eve-Mary parallelism as well.

Though Paul has little to say about Mary, it is he who develops at length the image of Jesus as the second Adam (Rom 5, 12-20; 1 Cor 15, 20-22). Jesus reverses the consequences of Adam's sin and begins a new era, really a new creation (2 Cor 5, 17; Gal 6, 15). He has made it possible for man, once again, to be "wise as to what is good and guileless as to what is evil" so that "the God of peace will soon crush Satan under your feet" (Rom 16, 19-20; the allusions to Genesis 3, 4—7, 15 are striking). With so much emphasis on the undoing of Adam's diso-bedience by Christ, it is hardly surprising that writers in the century following the period of the New Testament extended the parallel to include Mary. "For Eve, being a virgin and undefiled, conceiving the word that was from the serpent, brought forth disobedience and death; but the Virgin Mary, taking faith and joy, when the angel told her the good tidings ... answered, 'Be it to me according to thy word.'" These are the words of Justin Martyr (*Trypho* 100) writing around 160 A.D. The great bishop of Lyons, Irenaeus, a generation later, writes extensively along the same lines. Not only does Mary counter Eve's disobedience but she becomes "both to herself and to the whole human race the cause of salva-tion" (*Haer*. III. 22-34) and Eve's "advocate" (*Haer*. V. 19). Contemporaneously, Tertullian in Africa wrote: "What by that sex had gone into perdition by the same sex might be brought back to salvation. Eve had believed the serpent; Mary believed Gabriel; the fault which the one com-mitted by believing, the other by believing has blotted out" (*De Carn. Christ.* 17).

65

By the third century this understanding of Mary as a new or second Eve had become an integral part of Christian teaching about the mystery of salvation. For our study its particular interest lies in the rehabilitation of the female sex that it effects. If woman's avidity for knowledge had led to her punishment, and that of her posterity, another woman's wisdom reverses the situation: "Folly came from a woman, wisdom from a virgin" (Ambrose of Milan, *Commentary on Luke*). It is not just obedience but wisdom that Mary manifests, for she was free to reject the motherhood the angel invites her to accept, and indeed she does not, at first, show any inclination to acquiesce (Lk 1, 29-34), but when her questions are satisfied she utters the momentous "Let it be to me according to your word." In short, she exercises a true judgment, one that ultimately raises her to nearly divine status.

We may say then that Mary achieves Eve's goal. She comes to the knowledge of all things because she bears within her eternal wisdom, and the words of this wisdom she "kept in her heart" (Lk 2, 51). These considerations were to prepare the way for the ultimate identification of Mary with wisdom in the Middle Ages.

We have already noticed that early Christian writers found, in the Old Testament descriptions of wisdom, evidence of pre-Christian witness to the plurality of persons in God. The fact that in those passages divine wisdom is presented as a female hypostasis (or personality) was passed over, and this in turn was justified, not without reason (as we have also seen), on the grounds that the wisdom of God is also his Word. It is precisely as the *Word* of God (a masculine noun) that the prologue to the fourth gospel introduces the pre-existent Jesus, and this concept of the Christ as incarnate Word (and, correlatively, as incarnate wisdom) became a key element in the development of a rational Christological and trinitarian theology. However, it carried with it an inherent flaw: in two of the most important texts dealing with wisdom (Prv 8, 22; Sir 24, 9) it is explicitly stated that God *created* her. Now, as speculation about the nature of Jesus increased in the early centuries, that is, the attempt to explain how he could be both human and divine, these texts became more and more important. One group of theologians attached to an Alexandrian priest named Arius pointed out that if wisdom (the Word of God) was *created,* then it cannot be quite the same as God himself but a subordinate, semi-divine (because it is the *first* of all God's creatures and the instrument used for the creation of all others) being. Consequently, they argued, the Word of God, the second person of the Christian Trinity who took on human nature as Jesus Christ, is not truly equal to God. In terms of exegesis along strictly logical lines (and by this time the Christian world was deeply committed to Greek, and therefore to logical argument), the Arians were right. In terms of an understanding of Hebraic metaphor they were wrong. The writers of these biblical texts *did* think of wisdom as divine because they did not conceive of her as existing independently of God at all. If, as they did, they spoke of wisdom as being "created in the beginning," they merely meant something like "before God *did* anything he *thought* about it." Nevertheless, in a battle of metaphysics which rests its case on the univocal application of terms, the Arians had the better of the argument. The Arian position was indeed refuted in time, but on the basis of other biblical texts, and as a result of this conflict it became awkward to employ the wisdom passages in Christological and trinitarian discussion.

But surely such remarkable texts must refer to someone. If the someone was not the Son, the eternal Word or the Holy Spirit, but a creature, then the reference must be to the most exalted of creatures. The evidence, insofar as we can interpret it, seems to show that around the beginning of the seventh century, the text from Sirach 24 was being applied to virgins and martyrs in general. In other words, the saint, the individual who had certainly attained union with God, best answered the description of created wisdom. A little later, this passage was transferred to Mary, the virgin-saint *par excellence*. However, the application of the passage from Proverbs 8 to Mary was made without any such middle step, and we find it used of her in the liturgy of the feast of her nativity (September 8th) from the tenth century on. The development of the idea of Mary as the second Eve and as the wise virgin who reversed the consequences of the actions of the foolish virgin, to say nothing of the New Testament portrayal of Mary as the ark or seat of wisdom incarnate, had made easy this transition from a Christological to a Mariological exegesis of these wisdom texts, and as a consequence divine wisdom was restored to her natural sex.

Bibliography

L. Bouyer: *The Seat of Wisdom,* Chicago, 1965.

D. B. Capelle: "Les épîtres sapientiales des fêtes de la vierge," in *Quest Lit. Par* 27 (1946), 42-49.

R. Laurentin: *Queen of Heaven,* London & Dublin, 1956.

J. H. Newman: Letter to E. B. Pusey on the Eirenicon (Difficulties of Anglicans II).

H. Rahner: *Our Lady and the Church,* London, 1961.

II

Two legends were born in the Dark Ages which were to flourish in the high Middle Ages, both of which merit our attention because of the eminent position in which they place individual women. The women in these tales were reputed to have surpassed all other men of their times in knowledge and intelligence.

The first legend purports to tell the story of an Alexandrian maiden who suffered martyrdom for the faith under the emperor Maximinus (or Maxentius) in the early fourth century. This young lady, named Catherine, defied the emperor's order to sacrifice to the gods and presented herself before him as he was presiding at the ceremonies in Alexandria. She not only berated him but exposed all the fallacies in polytheism. Impressed, the emperor assembled together all the most distinguished philosophers in the realm and instructed them to persuade Catherine of the falsity of Christianity, for she would be a powerful asset to the pagan cause if she could be induced to abandon her faith. The result of the confrontation between Catherine and the philosophers was, however, not her conversion but theirs. Furthermore, even the empress and the emperor's most steadfast generals were won over to Christianity by Catherine. Only the emperor seemed to be able to hold out against her, and he had great difficulty in trying to find an effective means of putting her to death. As is usual in these martyr-legends, the stroke of the sword finally does the trick and in this particular story her remains are carried off by angels to Mount Sinai.

No trace of this legend has been discovered that is earlier than the eighth century, but the saint became enormously popular during the Middle Ages and, what is remarkable in an age where all learning was in the hands of men—celibates at that—she became the patroness of philosophers and theologians.

Catherine of Alexandria never existed and her name was officially removed from the calendar of Roman saints on July 9, 1969, but for six hundred years a woman, fictitious though she was, enjoyed the distinction of representing the apogee to which the human mind might aspire.

In all probability St. Catherine is not a complete myth but an example of how a collective sense of guilt can attempt to ease itself of its burden. In the latter part of the fourth century and the early years of the fifth century there was a remarkable woman in Alexandria whose name

71

was Hypatia. According to the historians of that era, "she was so learned that she surpassed all the philosophers of her time, and she assumed the direction of the school of Platonic thought which Plotinus had left as his legacy." Here indeed is the prototype of Catherine, barring the important fact that Hypatia was not a Christian. Hypatia met her death, a brutally violent one, at the hands of a Christian mob which resented the influence she had on the civil governor. She was a martyr, but to the virtues of paganism of which there were not a few examples in the philosophical circles of that period.

The murder of Hypatia outraged the conscience of the Christian world outside Alexandria (at least the historian Socrates tells us so), and we can readily imagine that the Alexandrians began to feel shame and guilt as a consequence. How could this be expiated? How other than by canonizing the woman they had destroyed? That this in fact did happen cannot be proven, but there is strong support for the assumption in the circumstance that not long after the tragic event a letter was fabricated, by some person or group of persons, purporting to be a communication from Hypatia to Cyril the patriarch of Alexandria. In this letter Hypatia speaks of her conversion to Christianity. Obviously this was the first necessary step, and who can object that it is a long one from a baptized Hypatia to a canonized Catherine when the former then fits the image of the latter so perfectly?

The other legend was probably a century in the making, since it seems to have grown out of the troubled conditions of Rome and the papacy in the tenth century. As a full-blown story it does not really appear for three centuries, and by that time a number of colorful details have crept in to give it a saucy verisimilitude. According to the legend a young girl born in England but reared in Mainz (her name is sometimes given as Agnes) is taken off to Athens by a wandering scholar who had fallen in love with her. In order to facilitate their amorous and scholarly pursuits, Agnes becomes "John" and passes for a man to all the world but her lover. Moreover, she makes such progress in learning that "no one could be found her equal." She and her lover move on to Rome where "John" excels in the Trivium (the formal study of grammar, rhetoric and logic) and attracts as *disciples* "great teachers." Finally, her reputation catapults her into the papacy and she reigns as pope for two years, one month and four days (855-858). Having successfully concealed her sex for so long a time and even her pregnancy, "John" is revealed to all for what she is by the sudden and unexpected birth of her child while she is on her way from St. Peter's to St. John Lateran in state procession. According to the most common version of the legend she dies in giving birth, thus eliminating further problems, but another version has her withdrawing to a convent to do penance for the rest of her life. In this account the child to whom she gave birth grows up to become bishop of Ostia, and with true filial piety he buries her in the cathedral of his suburban see.

The legend enjoyed great vogue from the thirteenth century to the time of the Reformation. No one seems to have thought it an unlikely story, and at least three popes could not have found it embarrassing since they made no effort to remove the portrait of Pope John (Joanna) which had been placed in the cathedral of Siena, where each of them had sat as archbishop before assuming the papal tiara (Pius II, Pius III, and Marcellus II). One writer at the beginning of the sixteenth century found in the election of Pope Joan evidence that divine providence wished to make clear that women are not inferior to men! This astonishingly modern view was proposed by Olivetanus (Marius Equicola d'Alveto) in his book *On Women*.

Careful historical research over the past three hundred years has shown that Pope Joan is a fiction. During the tenth century, however, one family, the Crescentii, dominated Roman politics, and one female member of that family, Marozia, reigned supreme: wife of the king of Italy, mistress of the pope (Sergius III), judge and jailer of the next pope (John XX), and mother of a third pope (John XXI). It was at this time that a contemporary chronicler wrote that "Roman power was subjugated to a woman," and this, in all likelihood, is the seed from which grew the florid legend of Pope Joan.

Once again, it is not the facts but the myths or legends that are important to our study. We can fathom today the origins of these legends, but that does not explain their great popularity. Does it not seem obvious that Western man of the Middle Ages *wanted* a woman as his ideal philosopher? Does it not also seem that in the minds of many the time had come for suggesting—tongue in cheek of course—that a woman might occupy the highest post in Christendom? When the Council of Constance convened (1414) and John Huss listed among his propositions the "fact" that the Roman Church was "deceived" in the person of "Agnes," none of the Council fathers bothered to refute him. This suggests that many of the Council fathers had already anticipated the views of Olivetanus and found them acceptable. In terms of today's interest in validating the official ministry of women in the Church, the silence of the fathers of Constance is something to be considered. They did not know the *facts,* but they did not seem to feel that the evidence of a female bishop of Rome destroyed the fabric of their belief in the Christian Church.

Bibliography

G. Bardy: "Catherine d'Alexandrie," *DHGE* II, 1504.

E. R. Chamberlain: *The Bad Popes,* New York, 1969.

L. Durrell: *Pope Joan,* London, 1960.

F. Vernet: Jeanne (La Papesse) *DAFC* 2, 1253-70.

III

It will be remembered that the controversy
with the Arians resulted in an unequivocal affirmation by the Church that the Son, the second
person of the Christian Trinity, was of the same
nature as the Father and uncreated. In just about
a century another controversy was raging throughout the Christian world. The patriarch of Constantinople, Nestorius, was preaching that the
human nature of Jesus was not so physically
united to the eternal divine Word that it would
be proper to speak of Mary as being the mother
of God; she was only the mother of the man
Jesus, the mother of the Christ whom God took
unto himself as his Son. Just as Arius was condemned at the Council of Nicaea (325 A.D.),
Nestorius was condemned at the Council of Ephesus (431 A.D.). There would be another important Council deliberation (at Chalcedon in
451) to reaffirm the integrity of Christ's human
nature, but we may say that with the rejection of
Nestorianism the Christian world had sealed its
conviction in the divinity of Jesus Christ.

77

Now these facts are of great importance toward understanding the development of Mariology in the Church. We have already seen that long before Nicaea or Ephesus Mary had assumed a significant role in Christian theology: she was the ark or seat of the incarnate Lord, the wise virgin who cooperated in our salvation and undid the work of Eve; she was the symbol of the Church as mother of all the faithful. Now, however, with the settlement of the Christological disputes, her stature increased and for two closely related reasons. The affirmation of the divinity of Jesus in the wake of the acrimonious debates which had divided Christendom tended to veil his humanity, despite the remedial effort made at Chalcedon. In order to protect the concept of his divinity, the fact that Jesus was also a man was barely acknowledged, and a Christology was developed which really made of him, as modern theologians realize, a psychological freak. In terms of the ordinary man who did not understand the subtleties whereby theologians preserved, in theory, the dual nature of Jesus, the Savior became as remote, as awesome and often as terrifying as his heavenly Father. It was not easy for medieval man to feel comfortable in the presence of the ruler of the universe (Christus Pantocrator), the appointed judge of mankind. We find this reflected in the sermons of one of the greatest preachers of the twelfth century, St. Bernard: Jesus is the all-powerful mediator between God and ourselves, he said, "but his divine majesty fills men with reverential awe. In him humanity seems to be absorbed by the divinity."

With Jesus almost inaccessible, to whom could the Christian turn with his or her prayers of petition except to his mother who, although she had borne the Son of God and was indeed called mother of God, remained nonetheless a human being? Mary becomes in medieval Christian piety, and in Roman Catholic piety up to very recent times, the favorite intercessor for man. She is the accessible one. To quote St. Bernard again, "Our Lady being altogether a creature like ourselves allows us to have complete confidence that with her we shall one day enter heaven."

But in filling the vacuum left by a distanced Christ, Mary also becomes a more exalted person herself. The more awesome her son becomes, the more wonderful must she herself be reckoned, and consequently, though she is "altogether a creature like ourselves," she cannot be an *ordinary* creature.

Now we have already seen how in the tenth century and earlier the passages from the wisdom books began to be applied to the virgin-mother, and we noted that this accommodation was based on the conviction that God had chosen her "from

the beginning" to be the mother of his Son.
Further, as noted again above, earlier than this
Mary is described as a new Eve and as the throne
of the Lord. Consider then what special qualities
she must have to be all these things. If she is the
Lord's throne, she must be adorned with the
finest gold, "gold" which does not corrupt. If she
is a new Eve, then she must, like Eve before the
fall, be completely innocent and not subject to
death. If she is the eternally determined mother
of God's Son, then she must, in the divine mind
and plan, be free of any taint which could mar
the dignity of that son whose flesh would be hers.

In these considerations we have the basis for
two affirmations about Mary which were eventually to become defined dogmas of the Roman
Catholic Church: that she was immaculately conceived, and that she was assumed, bodily, into
heaven. One can understand how these doctrines
would never have been developed if Nestorius
had triumphed rather than the fathers at Ephesus,
for if Mary was simply the mother of the man
Jesus, whose human nature was *appropriated* by
the divine Word but not united to it at the very
core of its reality as Nestorius held, then there
would be no particular reason why she should be
sinless and incorruptible. She would in that case
have been thought of simply as the mother of
someone *adopted by* God as his Son, and not as
the mother of someone *born* God in human flesh

(*her* flesh, since the doctrine of virgin birth precluded any human father and therefore the inheritance of any human qualities not his mother's).

The solemn proclamations of Mary's immaculate conception and bodily assumption represent the culmination of centuries of increasing devotion to the mother of God. The immaculate conception was not defined until 1854 and the assumption less than a quarter of a century ago, but these ideas appear in Christian literature as early as the fourth century (St. Ephraem the Syrian in the one case and St. Epiphanius of Cyprus in the other). Both were accepted teaching before the Reformation. Why was it then not until modern, indeed recent times, that the Roman Catholic Church gave them dogmatic status?

A principal argument used by Pope Pius XII in the bull proclaiming the assumption an article of faith is the desire and unanimity of the faithful, that is, the universal agreement among Catholics that this teaching is part of Christian revelation and the express wish that it be formally ratified as such. Such an argument was also employed by Pope Pius IX with regard to the immaculate conception. Both these popes solicited the views of the bishops of the Church throughout the world and through the bishops those of the faithful in general. The overwhelming positive response guaranteed popular support for these definitions (a certain amount of misgiving could be detected in the writings of some theologians), and it is this popular appeal which deserves our consideration here.

C. G. Jung has called attention to the "maternal character" of the Catholic Church, something he sees proven in her willingness to allow "the tree" which grows out of her matrix "to develop according to its own laws." This was especially true of the medieval Church and, to the extent that it was affected by the Church, of medieval society as well. But the maternalism of the medieval world, so well expressed by the position held by Mary in Christian piety, collapsed with the Reformation. Protestantism, Jung remarks, "is committed to the paternal spirit." The Reformation, in turn, was followed by the Enlightenment, the age of rationalism or, as the philosophers would have it, the "age of reason." Reason and rationalism stand in contrast to feeling and intuition (characteristically "feminine" qualities). The Enlightenment, finally, was followed by the Industrial Revolution as a result of which Western man began to think of himself as master of the universe (aggression), at the same time that he was subjecting nature and his own kind to sterility and brutalization (repression). But a pendulum can only swing so far in one direction. I suggest that what we see in the middle of the nineteenth century is the beginning of a reverse swing which today has gone very far—

but not all the way—in the opposite direction: a swing back toward the cultivation of the feminine spirit with the difference that the new age of woman will not be established without her active participation. Professor Jung hailed the proclamation of the assumption as the most important religious event since the Reformation. In criticizing the Protestant critics of the papal bull he credits the Catholic Church with having recognized, before the Protestant churches, "the signs of the times" which point to the imminent equality of the sexes and the need for a metaphysical anchor in the form of a "divine" woman by which woman's equality is guaranteed. I think we might say that the earlier definition of the immaculate conception was the first evidence of the signs of the times and the first move made since the end of the Middle Ages to redress the imbalance created by rationalistic male authoritarianism.

Bibliography

Y. M. Congar: *Christ, Our Lady, and the Church*, Westminster, Md., 1957.

H. de Lubac: *The Eternal Feminine*, London, 1971.

C. G. Jung: *Answer to Job*, London, 1954.

IV

From the time that the Middle Ages were drawing to a close until well into the seventeenth century, Western man was obsessed by another female image: that of the witch. Belief in the existence of witches or sorceresses is, of course, very ancient and not improbably a distorted memory of primitive matriarchal society and its priestesses. What distinguishes the obsession to which reference is made here was its relentless and savage persecution of anyone suspected of witchcraft. Perhaps we have only to look at the period to understand the phenomenon (though there were many diverse factors at work): this was a time of drastic change and social upheaval. The old medieval structures were giving way to new ones based on commerce and colonialism. The uniform presence of one Church throughout Europe was dispelled by a series of religious wars. Periods of great change are periods of unrest and uneasiness; the disappearance of the familiar creates suspicion and mistrust. Scapegoats are usually sought and found. In this case the witch was certainly one. The profile of the witch suggests why she was chosen. She was a woman, and although patriarchal society had reduced woman's role to one of mere domesticity, we have seen how much power the image of woman still exerted on the minds of men. As virgin-mother of God this image could be accepted and, indeed, desired (although in the period we are considering, that image too was greatly reduced in significance) but otherwise it could be feared. The witch, moreover, was a woman with special knowledge, special wisdom, and this made her a particular object of suspicion and resentment. Her knowledge, after all, was forbidden knowledge, and so she resembles no one so much as the unredeemed Eve. She is the opposite of the second Eve who had erased the first Eve's sin. Finally, and here too the parallel with Eve is valid (at least in terms of the Christian exegesis of Genesis), she is Satan's familiar. This meant that she was Satan's whore, and it was believed that copulation with Satan was the principal event of the witches' sabbath. In this respect the witch was also the antithesis of the virgin-mother.

But the witch and the virgin are both images of woman, and perhaps it is not without significance that the prosecution of witches was most intense and long-lasting in those countries where the virgin-mother was also pushed very far into the background. The two faces of woman, which, when superimposed on one another, reveal the ancient visage of the great mother goddess of earliest times, aroused the hostility of a world in ferment, and the angry furor was calmed only when the sons of the "Enlightenment," confident of their victory over the forces of ignorance and superstition, forced her to wear the mask of the "goddess of reason." And it was this ostensible victory which was followed, in less than a century, by the definition of the immaculate conception!

In our present age of ferment it is, of course, "male chauvinism," the "Protestant ethic" and the technology born of pure reason which are under attack, and it is difficult to predict what society will be like a hundred years from now. The role of woman has already changed greatly and, in doing so, seems to have emptied the old female religious symbols of their dynamism. A symbol, after all, is most powerful when it expresses subconscious reality or when it represents a taboo. Professor Jung, as we saw, felt that the equality of woman had to be tied to a concrete, personal, "divine woman," yet it seems very unlikely that the women most active today in pressing for those reforms which, to them, would represent true female equality would agree with him. Moreover, the whole direction of serious thought about the nature and reality of God in the past few decades has been away from the notion of "person" as traditionally understood, and if the idea of personality is eschewed, so too is that of sexuality.

However, theologians and philosophers are not the only people who think or write about God. The artist has always made his contribution, and it is interesting to note that one writer of our time has produced a challenging work in which, apparently, God is presented as a woman. I refer to Edward Albee's play *Tiny Alice*. It is rather like a parable. There are only five protagonists (six, when understood), and they are all concerned in a transaction (the transfer of a very large amount of money) between Miss Alice and the emissaries of the Catholic Church (a cardinal and his youngish secretary "Brother Julian"). One of Miss Alice's requirements is that Brother Julian come and take up residence in her home. In the great salon of her home there is a model of the mansion itself. We learn, as the drama progresses, that everything which happens in the mansion is also happening in the model. The mansion and its occupants *appear* to belong to the realm of reality (not to the realm of "make-believe" which the model house, the doll house, as it were, represents). But do they? We learn that these people really have no meaning apart from the model and its invisible inhabitant, Tiny Alice. Albee seems to be saying that God (Tiny Alice) is real because he (she) is make-believe, and *our* "reality," removed from make-believe, is shabby, pitiful and even absurd. Further, if the only reality with meaning is make-believe, and the only meaningful world a veritable doll's house, then God must be a woman, for a doll's house is the plaything of a girl. Perhaps Albee's theme is to be likened to Shakespeare's line: "All the world's a stage, and all the men and women merely players" (*As You Like It,* Act II, Scene 7), but he has laced it with contemporary existentialist views and one of his own. The nonexistent God of the absurd world in which we find ourselves can only be thought of as a woman. She is the antithesis of the goddess of reason because the world, which is hers, is a piece of nonsense, a construction of childish, feminine whim.

Perhaps (you will forgive me for using this word so often but in these matters there can only be opinions) *Tiny Alice* marks the same kind of turning point—unrecognized at the time—as did the enthronement of the goddess of reason in the profaned cathedral of Notre Dame. If people in general are not persuaded that the notion of God precludes personality, another century may witness a cyclic reaction to current trends and revive the image of an unequivocally male deity. Albee's *Tiny Alice* suggests à woman's world (the emergence of which seems possible) just as, according to Jung, Protestant Christianity suggested a man's. The dominance of one sex over the other will always be reflected in popular religion as long as it flourishes.

Bibliography

E. Albee: *Tiny Alice,* New York, 1970 (first published 1965).

H. W. Richardson: *Nun, Witch, Playmate,* New York, 1971.